Roald Dahl's
EVEN MORE REVOLTING RECIPES

Introduced by Felicity Dahl · Illustrated by Quentin Blake
Photographs by Jan Baldwin · Recipes by Lori-Ann Newman

To Roald's grandchildren and to my grandchildren - F.D.

Sophie
Clover
Luke
Phoebe
Chloe
Billy
Ned
Edie
Oscar

Max

Samuel

COOK'S NOTES

These recipes are for the family to enjoy making together.
Some could be dangerous without the help of an adult. Children,
please have an adult with you when you are using knives,
handling anything hot or using a food processor.

All measurements are given in metric.

EVEN MORE REVOLTING RECIPES
A RED FOX BOOK 978 0 099 41712 5

First published in Great Britain by Jonathan Cape,
an imprint of Random House Children's Publishers UK

Jonathan Cape edition published 2001
Red Fox edition published 2002

7 9 10 8 6

Text © Felicity Dahl and Roald Dahl Nominee Ltd, 2001
Illustrations © Quentin Blake, 2001
Photographs © Jan Baldwin, 2001

The right of Felicity Dahl, Quentin Blake and Jan Baldwin to be identified as the author, illustrator and
photographer of this work has been asserted in accordance with the Copyright, Designs and Patents Act 1988

Red Fox Books are published by Random House Children's Publishers UK,
61-63 Uxbridge Road, London W5 5SA,
a division of The Random House Group Ltd,
in Australia by Random House Australia (Pty) Ltd,
20 Alfred Street, Milsons Point, Sydney, NSW 2061, Australia,
in New Zealand by Random House New Zealand Ltd,
18 Poland Road, Glenfield, Auckland 10, New Zealand,
and in South Africa by Random House (Pty) Ltd,
Endulini, 5A Jubilee Road, Parktown 2193, South Africa

THE RANDOM HOUSE GROUP Limited Reg. No. 954009
www.randomhousechildrens.co.uk

A CIP catalogue record for this book is available from the British Library.

Printed in Malaysia by Tien Wah Press [PTE]

Royalties from this book will be donated to The Roald Dahl Foundation whose
aims are to help in the areas of neurology, haematology and literacy.

Introduction

"Nose-bags on!" or "Grub's up!" was Roald's way of announcing that the next meal was ready. He would preside at the head of the table in a very large armchair with Chopper, his dog, sitting on the arm beside him eagerly awaiting the ration of Smarties that he would be given at the end of the meal.

Roald's fascination with food certainly started at a young age. I remember him describing the start of his holidays at his grandparents' house in Oslo. His maiden aunts would be sitting on the veranda with large bowls of multer, a very special yellow blackberry native to Norway. Each of his aunts would be holding a needle and very carefully, they would examine each berry to see if a little worm was inside and yes, with a needle, they would make a stab and remove it. Roald said that the worms were not stupid. They were always in the sweetest and tastiest of berries.

His mother kept every letter he ever wrote to her from boarding school neatly tied in small bundles with pink ribbon like barristers' briefs. In these letters he was constantly asking her to send him food. Food that was not always easy to post. Can you imagine asking your mother to send you raw eggs?

"Thanks awfully, for your letter, and the eggs and the foot stuff. One egg was broken, so we had to throw it away but all the rest were fine. I had two of them poached last night for supper. And that foot powder is jolly good, I put some in this morning."

I hope not *in* the poached eggs!

He also asked her to send him a Primus stove to cook these raw ingredients on. Why? Well, I think the following extract will tell you:

"You see we are'nt allowed to cook supper on the fire on weekdays. But Michael and I had put a small tin of Peasoup in front of the fire to heat – one hour before

supper, which was quite within the law. When I came to take it off, the tin was bulging at both ends, hellish pressure inside owing to the steam of the boiling soup. I covered it with an umbrella and pierced it from behind – then took away the umbrella and stood at a safe distance; an enormous jet of steam and pea soup shot out, and continued to shoot for about 2 minutes – all over the study, the place was covered with condensing pea-soup."

As I continued to read these letters, did I find the seeds of the ideas that he later developed in his stories? Here is another extract. What do you think?

"Yesterday we had a lecture on China, it was jolly good, and the person described a Chinese Doctor, and said their prescriptions for flu was generally as follows:
A Rats tail
A snake
Chickens legs
Grass
Ashes of paper
Tiger bone-tea
And the shavings of Rhinoceros Horn"

Surely, this was the original draft of the centipede's song in *James and the Giant Peach*?

I hope that the recipes in this book will inspire you to be as inventive with your cooking as Roald was with his. I certainly hope that they will not make you suffer from indigestion as he did on 25th January 1930 when he wrote to his mother:

"Thanks awfully for the Tablets. I took some a few times and the indigestion has stopped now, they are jolly good."

FELICITY DAHL, GIPSY HOUSE 2001

Contents

The Royal Breakfast
for growing giants

During the next twenty minutes, a whole relay of footmen were kept busy hurrying to and from the kitchen carrying third helpings and fourth helpings and fifth helpings of fried eggs and sausages for the ravenous and delighted BFG.

THE BFG

MAKES 1

You will need:

small frying pan
large appetite

1 tsp oil
3 cocktail sausages
3 baby mushrooms
1 piece of back bacon,
* cut into strips*
1 cherry tomato
3 quail eggs
1 piece of toast
butter

1 Heat frying pan.

2 Add 1 tsp oil to warm pan.

3 Put sausages into pan and brown all over. When the sausages are nearly done, add the mushrooms and cook.

4 Add bacon to pan and cook to desired crispness.

5 Slice cherry tomato in half and add – cut side down – to pan. Cook for 2 minutes and carefully turn over.

6 Crack quail eggs into pan and fry until just cooked, but yolk is still soft (about 3 minutes).

7 While eggs are cooking, toast bread, butter it, and slice into 3 pieces.

8 Carefully slide everything onto a plate and eat immediately.

Hot-house Eggs

Nothing could be simpler or sillier than this recipe, but for some mysterious reason children love it. We always called it Hot-house Eggs, don't ask me why.

ROALD DAHL'S COOKBOOK

Use any type of egg for this recipe. If you are using an ostrich egg, the hole will need to be much bigger, but if you have a nematode egg, which is only 0.02mm, you will only need to make a pinprick in the bread.

You will need:

6cm pastry cutter
frying pan
1 slice of thickly cut bread
½ tbsp oil
1 tbsp butter
1 egg

1 Stamp out a hole in the bread with the pastry cutter.

2 Heat frying pan.

3 Add half the oil and butter to the pan.

4 When frothing add bread and cutout bit to pan.

5 Fry until golden brown and then flip over.

6 Carefully crack the egg into the hole and fry until cooked. If you like your eggs well done, you can flip the whole thing over and cook on the other side for about 30 seconds with the remaining butter and oil.

7 Serve with cutout bit.

The Hotel Breakfast

Breakfast was the best meal of the day in our hotel, and it was all laid out on a huge table in the middle of the dining-room from which you helped yourself. There were maybe fifty different dishes to choose from on that table.

BOY

A slightly simpler version...

SERVES 2

You will need:

25cm nonstick frying pan with ovenproof handle or an ovenproof dish

6 rashers of smoked back bacon

5 eggs

salt and pepper

2 tbsp milk

1 Heat the oven to 200°C/400°F/gas mark 6.

2 Slice bacon.

3 Fry until it starts to crisp.

4 Mix eggs, salt, pepper and milk.

5 Add to pan. (If you are using an ovenproof dish, place all ingredients in the dish and put in the oven.)

6 Don't stir.

7 Leave on the heat for 1 minute.

8 Put in the oven until the whole thing is puffed up and golden on top (about 15 minutes).

9 Turn it out onto a plate and eat.

NB. If an ovenproof dish is used for this recipe, The Hotel Breakfast will take 20-25 minutes to cook in the oven.

Hornets Stewed in Tar

"I've eaten fresh mudburgers by the greatest cooks there are,
And scrambled dregs and stinkbugs' eggs and
hornets stewed in tar..."
JAMES AND THE GIANT PEACH

You will need:

baking sheet
roasting tin
saucepan
1 adult

375g mixed seeds –
  pumpkin seeds,
  sunflower seeds,
  sesame seeds,
  poppy seeds and
  pine nuts (all shucked)
500g granulated sugar
375ml water
juice of ½ a lemon
1 tbsp black food colouring

1 Toast the seeds (apart from the poppy seeds) on a baking sheet in a 200°C/400°F/gas mark 6 oven for 10 minutes. Allow to cool.

2 Lightly butter the roasting tin and set to one side.

3 Put sugar and water in a saucepan over a low heat and stir until all the sugar has dissolved.

4 Turn the heat up and stop stirring. Be very careful, as boiling sugar is extremely hot. Stand back from the saucepan, but don't leave the kitchen because caramel always burns if you turn your back on it.

5 When it starts turning a beautiful golden colour (about 10 minutes), add the lemon juice and food colouring. Add it quickly and then move your hand away immediately, as it will spit and splutter like a live volcano.

6 Quickly stir in all the seeds and pour into the roasting tin. Leave to cool and harden. When it is completely cold, turn it out and break it into bite-size chunks. Keep them in an airtight container and they will remain delicious for days.

13

Pickled Spines of Porcupines

"I'm mad for crispy wasp-stings on a piece of buttered toast,
And pickled spines of porcupines. And then a gorgeous roast
Of dragon's flesh, well hung, not fresh – it costs a pound at most,
(And comes to you in barrels if you order it by post.)"

JAMES AND THE GIANT PEACH

To avoid a crisis in this recipe, when you are painting the black bits on the porcupine spines do so very lightly, and with only a tiny amount of the food colouring. If not, the spines go soggy and flop over like limp hair.

You will need:

electric whisk
*piping bag with a very
  small plain nozzle or
  a small plastic bag*
*2 baking sheets covered
  in nonstick baking
  parchment*

4 egg whites
225g caster sugar
1 tsp cornflour
1 tsp black food colouring

1 Heat the oven to 130°C/250°F/gas mark 1.

2 Whisk egg whites to 'stiff peak' stage.

3 While beating, gradually add the caster sugar a little bit at a time. Whisk until it's as stiff as the stiffest thing in the world, and then quickly whisk in the cornflour.

4 Now pipe 15 thin strips about 30 cm long onto one of the baking sheets. If you don't have a piping bag just put the mixture into a small plastic bag and snip a tiny bit off the corner to squeeze out of. It doesn't matter if they are not perfectly straight, as these porcupine spines are pickled.

5 Make one big mound for the porcupine's body with the leftover mixture and place on the other baking sheet. Place both sheets in the oven.

6 Bake the spines for about 30 minutes, and then take them out and leave on one side to cool. Leave the body in for a further 45 minutes or until the parchment peels away from the porcupine.

7 When the body is ready, take it out and allow to cool (about 10-15 minutes), then make tiny little holes for the spines.

8 Paint 2 cm long strips of black on the spines, leaving 2 cm strips unpainted in between. Stick the spines into the little holes. The food colouring will soften the spines fairly quickly so this creation has a 10 minute viewing time before you have to eat it.

Doc Spencer's Pie

Not exactly like Doc Spencer's wife makes for him, but easier to eat if you're stuck somewhere in the wild with no knife and can't find Mrs Doc Spencer.

MAKES 6

You will need:

pastry brush
baking sheet

4 slices of ham
4 hard-boiled eggs
1 tbsp mayonnaise
2 tbsp grated
  Cheddar cheese
salt
freshly ground
  black pepper
1 pack filo pastry
40g butter, melted
sesame seeds

1 Preheat oven to 200°C/400°F/gas mark 6.

2 Roughly chop ham.

3 Roughly chop eggs.

4 Mix together ham, eggs, mayonnaise, Cheddar cheese, salt and pepper.

5 Cut a sheet of filo pastry in half widthways. Lay one piece on top of the other.

6 Brush with melted butter. Put 2 tbsp of egg and ham mix onto the pastry and carefully roll into a cigar shape, folding in the sides so that it is safely sealed.

7 Brush the top with melted butter and sprinkle with sesame seeds. Continue until all the mixture is used up, or you lose interest (the rest can be a delicious sandwich filling).

8 Bake in preheated oven for 15-20 minutes or until golden brown.

9 Allow to cool for 8 minutes before you eat it otherwise you'll burn your tongue.

Very carefully, I now began to unwrap the greaseproof paper
from around the doctor's present, and when I had finished,
I saw before me the most enormous and beautiful pie in
the world. It was covered all over, top, sides, and
bottom, with a rich golden pastry.

DANNY THE CHAMPION OF THE WORLD

Pishlets

They had a splendid effect upon the Pelican, for after he had put one of them into his beak and chewed it for a while, he suddenly started singing like a nightingale. This made him wildly excited because Pelicans are not song-birds.

THE GIRAFFE AND THE PELLY AND ME

You know that enormously annoying feeling you get when you know you want to eat something, and you rack your brains but still can't decide? Next time this feeling strikes you down, don't stop to think, just run into the kitchen without delay, put on an apron, and make up a batch of Pishlets.

You will need:

shallow roasting tin
saucepan

170g butter
150g demerara sugar
1 tsp bicarbonate of soda
1 apple
1 pear
200g oats
75g raisins
75g dried cherries

1 Grease a shallow roasting tin.

2 Heat the oven to 180°C/350°F/gas mark 4.

3 Melt the butter, demerara sugar and bicarbonate of soda in a saucepan over a low heat.

4 While they are melting, peel the apple and pear and chop them into bite-size chunks.

5 Add the oats, raisins, dried cherries, apple and pear to the saucepan and mix well.

6 Spoon into the roasting tin and spread evenly.

7 Place in the oven and cook for about 25-30 minutes until golden on top.

8 Let it cool down and then cut into squares.

19

Plushnuggets

*There were Gumtwizzlers and Fizzwinkles from China,
Frothblowers and Spitsizzlers from Africa, Tummyticklers and
Gobwangles from the Fiji Islands and Liplickers and <u>Plushnuggets</u>
from the Land of the Midnight Sun.*

THE GIRAFFE AND THE PELLY AND ME

MAKES 12

You will need:

7cm pastry cutter
rolling pin
pastry brush
baking tray

2 bananas
2 tsp maple syrup
2 tsp olive oil
1 pack puff pastry
  (preferably all butter)
1 egg yolk

1 Squish the bananas with a fork and add maple syrup and olive oil.

2 Cut a 7 cm wide circle out of the pastry with a pastry cutter.

3 Roll the circle out so it is 1.5 cm bigger.

4 Put a blob of the banana mix in the middle and lift up the edges to squash them together.

5 Use up the rest of the pastry in the same way.

6 Put in the fridge.

7 Heat oven to 200°C/400°F/gas mark 6.

8 When oven is at correct temperature, brush plushnuggets with yolk and put in the oven on the baking tray for about 20 minutes or until they are golden.

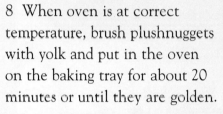

9 Allow them to cool for about 10 minutes before you eat them, as the middle remains very hot.

Strawberry Bonbons

The kind you can't find in any sweet shop...

On the way to school and on the way back we always passed the sweet-shop. No we didn't, we never passed it. We always stopped. We lingered outside its rather small window gazing in at the big glass jars full of Bull's-eyes and Old Fashioned Humbugs and Strawberry Bonbons and Glacier Mints and Acid Drops and Pear Drops and Lemon Drops and all the rest of them.

BOY

You will need:

food processor
fine sieve
small saucepan
tray
nonstick baking
   parchment
1 adult
toothpicks

200g strawberries
100g granulated sugar
8 tbsp water
¼ tsp liquid glucose

1 Liquidise half of the strawberries and then push the purée through a very fine sieve, so that you don't have any of the seeds left.

2 Put the sugar, water and liquid glucose into a small saucepan and stir over a low heat until all the sugar is melted.

3 Turn the heat up and stop stirring.

4 While this is cooking make sure that the remainder of the strawberries are completely dry. Place a sheet of nonstick baking parchment onto a tray in preparation for the next stage.

5 When the sugar and water starts to turn golden (about 5 minutes), turn off the heat and stir in 2 tbsp of the puréed strawberry. Be very careful when you add the purée, as it will spit, and it is extremely hot.

6 Allow the mixture to cool for 10 minutes, and then put the whole strawberries onto toothpicks and dip into the caramel. Place on the non-stick baking parchment to cool. These will start weeping after about 15 minutes, so don't delay too long before eating!

Tummyticklers

There were Gumtwizzlers and Fizzwinkles from China, Frothblowers and Spitsizzlers from Africa, <u>Tummyticklers</u> and Gobwangles from the Fiji Islands and Liplickers and Plushnuggets from the Land of the Midnight Sun.

THE GIRAFFE AND THE PELLY AND ME

This won't make you itchy like a toe tickle – it's a delicate delight to soothe a hungry stomach. It's really like a toasted cheese stack, but don't stop at cheese – you can put in any fillings you like, even sweet ones, and you can have as many layers of tortillas in your Tummyticklers as your mouth can fit around. (This may require some training – nightly mouth stretching.)

You will need:

1 massive frying pan
1 adult

3 soft flour tortillas
1 scant tbsp grainy
  mustard
1 tbsp mayonnaise
6 tbsp grated Cheddar
  cheese
2 finely sliced spring
  onions
½ tbsp olive oil
freshly ground pepper

1 Spread mustard over one tortilla and mayonnaise over the other.

2 Sprinkle both with cheese.

3 Scatter the spring onion over the one with mayonnaise. Stack one tortilla on top of the other and cover with the third tortilla.

4 Heat the massive frying pan, then add the oil.

5 Carefully transfer the stack of tortillas into the frying pan.

6 Cook on both sides over a medium heat until golden and crispy – about 2 minutes. An easy way of turning it over is to place a plate big enough to cover the whole thing over the frying pan and then turn everything upside down, so that you end up with it on the plate. Then slide it back into the pan so the other side can cook. Be careful when doing this as it is extremely hot.

7 Cut it into small slices like a cake and serve warm.

Boiled Slobbages

*"I often eat boiled slobbages. They're grand when served beside
Minced doodlebugs and curried slugs. And have you ever tried
Mosquitoes' toes and wampfish roes Most delicately fried?"*

JAMES AND THE GIANT PEACH

A rare delicacy – by far the best slobbages in the land.

NB. The sauce needs to be prepared an hour ahead, and the slobbages can be
prepared a few hours ahead and then reheated when you are ready to eat.

SERVES 3

You will need:

large saucepan
large bowl
colander
spatula
frying pan
6 vine-ripened tomatoes
6 basil leaves
1 whole mozzarella
  cheese
4 tbsp extra virgin
  olive oil
salt and pepper
2 eggs
130ml milk
¼ tsp nutmeg
170g plain flour

1 Chop tomatoes into small pieces.

2 Tear the basil leaves into small pieces.

3 Chop the mozzarella into small cubes.

4 Combine the tomato, mozzarella, basil, 3 tbsp of the olive oil, salt and pepper.

5 Let this stand at room temperature for about an hour.

6 Meanwhile, mix together eggs, milk, salt, pepper and freshly grated nutmeg.

7 Add the flour to the egg mixture. If it appears lumpy, use a whisk.

8 Let it rest in the fridge for 10 minutes.

9 Put a large pan of salted water on to boil.

10 Fill a large bowl with cold water.

11 When the water in the pan is boiling, hold the colander above the saucepan and pour the mixture into it, pushing it through with a spatula.

12 Simmer the slobbages for 2 minutes and then remove them with a slotted spoon and put them straight into the bowl of cold water.

13 When you are ready to eat, drain the slobbages and heat them in a frying pan with the remaining olive oil.

14 Add the tomato sauce, stir and serve.

Glumptious Globgobblers

To the Giraffe I gave a bag of Glumptious Globgobblers. The Globgobbler is an especially delicious sweet that is made somewhere near Mecca, and the moment you bite into it, all the perfumed juices of Arabia go squirting down your gullet one after the other.

THE GIRAFFE AND THE PELLY AND ME

The traditional globgobbler, made somewhere near Mecca, is a delicious sweet. This variety, made in a secret undercover location miles away from Mecca, is a mouth-watering savoury treat.

MAKES 24

You will need:

saucepan
food processor
frying pan
1 adult
kitchen paper

125g arborio rice
2 skinless and boneless
   chicken breasts
1 tbsp freshly grated ginger
1 tsp medium curry powder
1 clove of garlic, crushed
3 tbsp roughly chopped
   coriander
4 spring onions, sliced
4 tbsp sweetcorn
1/2 tsp salt
freshly ground black pepper
100ml light soy sauce
oil for deep-frying

1 Cook rice in 450ml of boiling salted water for 15 minutes and then rinse under cold running water until completely cold.

2 Place chicken breasts in food processor and blitz until smooth.

3 Add all other ingredients, apart from soy sauce and oil. Blitz again for about 30 seconds.

4 Heat oil – about 2 cm deep – in a frying pan. This would be the moment for an adult to help out.

5 While the adult is assisting you in the deep-frying department, rub a bit of cold oil on your hands and grab a walnut-sized piece of the glumptious mix. Roll it into a ball. Continue until all the mixture is used up.

6 Stand back and hand over the globgobblers to the deep-frying department. The head of this department will then fry them until golden brown all over.

7 Drain on kitchen paper and sprinkle lightly with salt. Use soy sauce as a dip.

Toad-in-the-Hole

"By golly!" he cried. "That'll be the very first thing we'll make in our new oven! Toad-in-the-hole!"
DANNY THE CHAMPION OF THE WORLD

I've never been lucky enough to see a toad in its hole, but
I'm sure this is just how it looks.

MAKES 4

You will need:

frying pan
apple corer
kitchen foil

250g minced beef or lamb
½ tbsp oil
½ onion
½ leek
½ carrot
½ stick of celery
1 tsp tomato purée
1 tbsp Worcestershire sauce
salt and pepper
4 baking potatoes
4 tbsp grated cheese
knob of butter

1 Heat the oven to 200°C/400°F/gas mark 6.

2 Finely chop all the vegetables.

3 In a frying pan, brown the mince.

4 Strain into a bowl, and return any liquid to the pan. Add the oil and fry the vegetables until light brown.

5 Put the mince back into the pan with the vegetables. Add the tomato purée, Worcestershire sauce, a pinch of salt and a few turns of black pepper.

6 Allow to cool.

7 While the mixture is cooling, use the apple corer to make two long holes in each potato. Keep the bits you take out of the middle and trim them so that you are left with 1 cm from each end.

8 Push the mince into the holes in each potato and plug them up with the 1 cm bits you have trimmed.

9 Wrap each potato in foil and bake for about $1\frac{1}{4}$ hours. After this time, unwrap the potatoes and place them back in the oven on top of the foil to crisp for a further 15 minutes. Take care when handling as they will be extremely hot.

10 Cut each potato in half, cover with the grated cheese, the knob of butter, a bit more salt and pepper and eat while hot.

Wonka's Whipple-Scrumptious Fudgemallow Delight

*"Wonka's Whipple-Scrumptious Fudgemallow Delight!" cried
Grandpa George. "It's the best of them all! You'll just love it!"*

CHARLIE AND THE CHOCOLATE FACTORY

The supreme queen of ice cream sauces!

You will need:

saucepan

1 adult

*large bowl of your
   favourite ice cream
   ready in the fridge*

60g dark chocolate

1 Cadbury's Crunchie

60g butter

80g dark brown sugar

150ml double cream

8 marshmallows

1 Break the chocolate and the Crunchie into large chunks and set to one side.

2 In a saucepan, over a low heat, melt together the butter, sugar and cream.

3 Stir until all the sugar has dissolved and then turn the heat up and continue stirring for 10 minutes. Be careful, as it gets very hot and can splutter. Use a very long wooden spoon or a tall adult with a long arm.

4 Turn the heat down again, and get your bowl of ice cream from the fridge.

5 Put the marshmallows, chocolate and Crunchie into the saucepan, stir around once and pour over your ice cream.

NB. You can keep the leftover sauce in the fridge and reheat in the microwave.

Hot Noodles made from Poodles on a Slice of Garden Hose

"For dinner on my birthday shall I tell you what I chose:
Hot noodles made from poodles on a slice of garden hose –
And a rather smelly jelly made of armadillo's toes.
(The jelly is delicious, but you have to hold your nose.)"

JAMES AND THE GIANT PEACH

SERVES 2-3

You will need:

slotted spoon
food processor
clingfilm
rolling pin
2 coat hangers
large saucepan

50g flat leaf parsley
2 large eggs
200g plain flour
1 tbsp olive oil
1 tbsp Parmesan
   cheese
salt and pepper

1 Bring a pan of water to the boil. Fill a large bowl with very cold water and have it ready next to the pan. When the water is boiling, drop the parsley into it – count to 5 and then take it out with a slotted spoon and drop straight into the bowl of very cold water.

2 Squeeze the parsley very hard – you want to get all the water out – and then place it on a paper towel and set aside.

3 Put the eggs and flour into the food processor and process for 2 minutes. You should have a soft but not sticky dough.

4 Take out of the machine and knead on a lightly floured surface for a couple of minutes. Cover with clingfilm and let it rest for 15 minutes.

5 After 15 minutes place about one quarter of the dough in the food processor with the parsley, and whizz until the parsley is completely mixed into the dough, and the dough has turned garden hose green. Take out and place on a floured surface. Using the rolling pin, roll it out as thinly as possible, and then cut into 4 cm wide strips to make your flattened garden hose.

6 Hang the strips over a coat hanger to dry out while you make the poodle noodles.

7 Roll out the poodle (the other batch of dough) as thinly as possible and then roll up like a swiss roll and slice very thinly.

8 Unravel these slices and hang on a coat hanger too. Allow to dry for 30 minutes.

9 Bring a very large saucepan of water to the boil and add 2 tsp of salt, then put the garden hose in and cook at a rapid boil for 3-5 minutes.

10 Take out with a slotted spoon and drain in a colander.

11 Put the noodles in the boiling water and cook for 2-5 minutes depending on the thickness of the dough. Drain into the colander with the garden hose in, and then put everything back into the saucepan, off the heat. Toss in the olive oil and some salt and pepper to taste.

12 Lay the garden hose onto a plate and top with the noodles and Parmesan.

Hot Dogs

"I crave the tasty tentacles of octopi for tea
I like hot dogs, I LOVE hot-frogs, and surely you'll agree
A plate of soil with engine oil's a super recipe.
(I hardly need to mention that it's practically free.)"
JAMES AND THE GIANT PEACH

No one can deny that hot dogs are one of the greatest things mankind has ever invented, BUT he made a mistake. No matter how hard you try, some of the ketchup or mustard always spills out in the end. This recipe is an essential for anyone who loves hot dogs but ends up with most of the filling on the carpet/in the dog's mouth/on the pavement/on the sparkling new trousers.

MAKES 8

You will need:

large bowl
roasting tin (for sausages)
weighing scales
rolling pin
small roasting tin
pastry brush

1 packet of bread
  dough mix
8 sausages
8 rashers of back bacon
  (only if you like it in
  your hot dog)
tomato ketchup
mustard (your favourite
  kind)
1 egg yolk

1 Preheat the oven to 200°C/400°F/gas mark 6

2 Follow instructions on side of bread mix, and make the dough.

3 While the dough is rising, cook the sausages in the oven. If you are using the bacon, wrap it around the sausages before cooking. When they are light brown (about 15 minutes) take them out and allow to cool.

4 When the dough has doubled in size, weigh out eight 70g pieces.

5 Roll each piece of dough to a 12 cm wide circle.

6 Place the sausage in the middle of the dough and spread with a small amount of ketchup and/or mustard.

7 Carefully roll it up, keeping it quite tight, and fold the sides in so that there is no chance of escape.

8 Do the same with the rest of the sausages. Place in the roasting tin.

9 Brush with the egg yolk and allow to rise again.

10 When they have doubled in size again (20-30 minutes), place in oven and cook for about 20-25 minutes or until golden.

11 Allow to cool for 5 minutes before eating – the waiting is the only difficult part of the recipe. Set an alarm clock and eat as soon as the bell goes.

Grobswitchy Cake

"It is a little bit like mixing a cake," the BFG said. "If you is putting the right amounts of all the different things into it, you is making the cake come out any way you want, sugary, splongy, curranty, Christmassy or grobswitchy. It is the same with dreams."

THE BFG

SERVES 8

You will need:

bowl
mixing bowl
electric whisk
20cm nonstick cake tin

4 tbsp soft brown sugar
1 tsp ground cinnamon
250g butter
150g caster sugar
2 eggs
300g sour cream
210g plain flour
70g self-raising flour
1 tsp bicarbonate of soda
1 cup chopped pecans
2 tbsp grobswitchies
   (also known as
   amber sugar
   crystals)

1   Heat oven to 170°C/325°F/gas mark 3.

2   Mix together soft brown sugar and cinnamon and put to one side.

3   In a mixing bowl, cream butter and sugar until pale and fluffy.

4   Add eggs one at a time, whisking after each addition.

5   Stir in the sour cream. Sift the plain flour, self-raising flour and bicarbonate of soda in together.

6   Add half the mixture to the cake tin.

7   Sprinkle in half the cinnamon and sugar mix, half the chopped pecans and half the grobswitchies.

8   Add the other half of the cake mix and then sprinkle the rest of the cinnamon and sugar, pecans and grobswitchies on the top.

9   Put in oven and cook for 1-1½ hours, or until a skewer comes out clean.

10   Allow to cool for about 15 minutes and then eat with some cream while still warm.

11   This cake keeps well for about a week.

NB. Grobswitchies remain hard even when cooked, so be careful if you have false teeth!

A Plate of Soil with Engine Oil

"I crave the tasty tentacles of octopi for tea
I like hot dogs, I LOVE hot-frogs, and surely you'll agree
A plate of soil with engine oil's a super recipe.
(I hardly need to mention that it's practically free.)"

JAMES AND THE GIANT PEACH

SERVES 6

You will need:

2lb loaf tin
mixing bowl
shallow roasting tin
deep serving dish

170g plain flour
150g soft brown sugar
50g cocoa powder
150ml milk
50g butter, melted
100g dark chocolate
55g soft brown sugar
400ml hot milk
cream

1 Grease the loaf tin.

2 Preheat the oven to 180°C/350°F/gas mark 4.

3 Mix the flour and the first amount of sugar with half the cocoa powder.

4 Beat in the milk and melted butter.

5 Break the chocolate into rough pieces and stir into the mixture.

6 Pour into the loaf tin.

7 Sprinkle the second amount of sugar and the other half of the cocoa powder over the top of the mixture.

8 Pour hot milk over it, place the loaf tin in a shallow roasting tin and bake for 1 hour 15 minutes. It is ready when the top feels crusty.

9 Carefully turn the whole thing out into a deep serving dish and eat it with cream while still hot.

NB. You can replace the dark chocolate with white chocolate if you prefer, or do a mixture of the two.

I find that old engine oil has a more refined taste than fresh. When engine oil is fresh it is more like caramel which doesn't go at all well with soil (not bad with fried ants though).

Luminous Lollies for Eating in Bed at Night

MAKES ABOUT 12

You will need:

food processor
small plastic/disposable
  cups
clingfilm
plastic forks
plastic spoons
luminous paint (the type
  you can paint on
  plastic)
paintbrush

1 large ripe mango,
  chopped
50g dried mango,
  chopped
2 tbsp icing sugar
1 tsp lemon juice

NB. You should prepare these well in advance, as they need a whole night to freeze.

1 Put all the ingredients into the food processor and whizz until smooth.

2 Fill the plastic cups to 1 cm below the top with the mango mix. Cover with clingfilm and place in the freezer overnight.

3 Paint the prong end of the forks and the bowl end of the spoons to a third of the way up the handle. Allow to dry completely.

4 Take one of the plastic cups out of the freezer and snip the top of the cup all around the edge at 1 cm intervals (you need to work quite quickly here so that you get to eat the lolly before it melts!). Tear down from the bits you have snipped so that all the sides of the cup are down.

5 Carefully place the frozen mango on a board and slice into 2 cm rounds.

6 Slip these over the non-painted bits of the spoons and forks, making sure the food doesn't touch the paint.

7 You can eat these straight away or cover and put back in the freezer for another night.

The Magic Green Crystal

Warning! These sacred treasures will be much in demand. Don't leave home without securing your lunchbox with an alarm and padlock. You can never be too careful when it comes to the magic green crystal.

You will need:

small saucepan
1 adult
baking tray, oiled

80g caster sugar
2 tbsp golden syrup
1 tbsp lemon juice
3 tbsp water
*½ tbsp green food
    colouring*
1 tsp bicarbonate of soda

1 Put the sugar, syrup, lemon juice and 3 tbsp of water into the saucepan. Start it on a low heat and stir until all the sugar has dissolved.

2 Turn the heat up and boil without stirring until it is a rich golden caramel brown (about 10 minutes).

3 Remove from the heat and quickly stir in the food colouring and then the bicarbonate of soda – it will froth up straight away.

4 Pour it onto the oiled baking tray and let it start to set.

5 Just before it hardens completely, cut it into diamonds with an oiled knife.

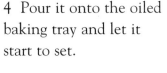

"Take a look, my dear," he said, opening the bag and tilting
it towards James. Inside it, James could see a mass of tiny green
things that looked like little stones or crystals.

JAMES AND THE GIANT PEACH

Nishnobblers

...there were <u>Nishnobblers</u> and Gumglotters and Blue Bubblers and Sherbet Slurpers and Tongue Rakers, and as well as all this, there was a whole lot of splendid stuff from the great Wonka factory itself.

THE GIRAFFE AND THE PELLY AND ME

Nishnobblers are made from tempered chocolate. Tempering is when you mix melted and solid chocolate together to make it shinier and more manageable. It is an indispensable skill to have in life, and you learn how to do it right here! Once you've got the hang of it, you'll be able to create masterful chocolate constructions to rival Willy Wonka's.

MAKES 6

You will need:

pyrex bowl
saucepan
30 x 25cm sheet of
*   bubble wrap*
7cm pastry cutter
pastry brush
100g good quality dark
*   chocolate*
100g good quality white
*   cooking chocolate*

1 Melt 70g of the dark chocolate in a pyrex bowl on the defrost setting in the microwave or over a saucepan of simmering water. When it is melted, stir the unmelted 30g into it until the whole lot is smooth.

2 Paint over the bubble wrap with the melted chocolate and place it in the fridge for 15 minutes.

3 Temper the white chocolate in the same way. (NB. White chocolate melts faster than dark chocolate, so you may want to let it cool a little before you start painting.) Spread it over the dark chocolate. Chill for 15 minutes.

4 Carefully peel the bubble wrap away from the chocolate and cut it into rounds with the pastry cutter.

Butter Gumballs

The sweet-shop of my dreams would be loaded from top to bottom with Sherbet Suckers and Caramel Fudge and Russian Toffee and Sugar Snorters and <u>Butter Gumballs</u> and thousands and thousands of other glorious things like that.
THE GIRAFFE AND THE PELLY AND ME

These make great presents for parents, as they can't talk for ages while they chew and chew and chew. The recipe makes enough for you to keep a small supply for yourself as well.

You will need:

*medium size heavy
    bottomed saucepan*
friends with strong arms
large tray
*nonstick baking
    parchment*
tin foil
plenty of time

1 tin condensed milk
2 tbsp demerara sugar
2 tbsp golden syrup
30g butter

1 Put all the ingredients into the saucepan and stir over a low heat until it becomes a beautiful toffee colour, and quite thick. This will take about 25-30 minutes, and it is important that you stir for the whole time, otherwise it will burn at the bottom.

2 Cover a large tray with nonstick baking parchment, and using 2 teaspoons, put teaspoon-size blobs of the mixture onto the paper, spaced well apart.

3 Allow the blobs to get completely cold and then shape into balls by rubbing them between your palms. If the mixture doesn't stay in shape it means that it needs to be cooked for a little longer, so head back to the stove and start stirring.

4 If you are going to give a few away as presents then cut squares of tin foil and wrap each Butter Gumball up like a Christmas cracker.

Tongue Rakers

...there were Nishnobblers and Gumglotters and Blue Bubblers and Sherbet Slurpers and <u>Tongue Rakers</u>, and as well as all this, there was a whole lot of splendid stuff from the great Wonka factory itself.
THE GIRAFFE AND THE PELLY AND ME

MAKES 1

You will need:

bowl, lightly greased
clingfilm
small saucepan
sieve
rolling pin
large baking sheet

1 packet of bread dough
  mix (whatever kind
  you like)
1 onion
2 cloves of garlic
20g butter
1 tsp salt
1 egg yolk
1 tsp rosemary
1/2 tsp coarse salt

1 Heat the oven to 200°C/400°F/gas mark 6.

2 Mix the bread dough according to the instructions on the packet. Knead for 8 minutes, and then place in a lightly greased bowl, cover with clingfilm and allow to rise until doubled in size (about 1 hour).

3 Finely chop the onion and garlic. Melt the butter in a small saucepan and add the chopped onion and the salt. Cover, and cook over a very low heat for 15 minutes or until soft. Add the garlic and cook for a further 2 minutes.

4 Next, drain the onion and garlic in a sieve over a bowl, and allow to cool.

5 When the dough has risen enough, add the cooled onion and garlic and knead again for 5 minutes. If the dough becomes sticky you may need to add a bit more flour – just enough to make it easy to knead.

6 Break off seven 30g pieces and one 180g piece.

7 Roll the biggest piece so that it is the length of 1½ pencils, and a little bit thicker than a pencil.

8 Place this onto the large baking sheet.

9 Roll all the other pieces to the same thickness but half the length, and then attach these (by squishing) to one end of the long piece – just like you see in the picture. If your baking sheet is too small to do such a big one, you can just make it smaller. Tongue Rakers of all sizes are delicious.

10 Brush the Tongue Raker with the egg yolk, and sprinkle with rosemary and coarse salt.

11 When the dough is well risen, bake until golden brown – about 20-25 minutes.

NB. You could use any leftover dough to make a loaf of bread. (This will probably take 30-35 minutes to cook.)

Lizards' Tails

*"I've eaten fresh mudburgers by the greatest cooks there are,
And scrambled dregs and stinkbugs' eggs and hornets stewed in tar,
And pails of snails and lizards' tails,
And beetles by the jar."*
JAMES AND THE GIANT PEACH

Prawnosaurus-Rex.
Roasted, grilled, curried or stewed, the base of the tail and toes are the best cuts.

MAKES 18

You will need:

food processor
mixing bowl
baking sheet, lightly greased
pastry brush

*400g raw prawns with the
  shell on (fresh or frozen)*
1 tbsp fresh mint
1 clove of garlic
3 spring onions

1 egg white
1 tsp cornflour
1 tsp sugar
salt and pepper
oil

For the dip:
2 tbsp fresh mint
½ mild chilli (de-seeded)
1 tbsp fish sauce
1 tsp sugar
juice of 2 limes

1 Defrost prawns completely if using frozen ones.

2 Cut off the tail bit at the end of the prawns and set aside in the fridge.

3 Peel the rest of the prawns and place in the food processor with the mint, garlic, spring onion, egg white, cornflour, sugar and a pinch of salt and pepper. Blitz.

4 Cover and chill in the fridge for 20 minutes.

5 Heat the grill.

6 Prepare the dip: roughly chop the mint, finely chop the chilli. Mix together the mint, chilli, fish sauce, sugar and lime juice. Cover and set aside.

7 Wet your hands and shape the prawn mix into tails (wetting your hands stops the mixture from sticking to you).

8 Place on a lightly greased baking sheet. Stick the prawn tails into the mixture down the middle of the tail. Brush each lizard's tail with oil and place under the grill for 5-7 minutes.

9 Eat with the dip, first removing the prawn tails.

Spitsizzlers

There were Gumtwizzlers and Fizzwinkles from China,
Frothblowers and <u>Spitsizzlers</u> from Africa, Tummyticklers and
Gobwangles from the Fiji Islands and Liplickers and Plushnuggets
from the Land of the Midnight Sun.

THE GIRAFFE AND THE PELLY AND ME

Even better than crisps!

You will need:

2 saucepans
colander
paper towels
large slotted spoon
*an adult to assist with
    the deep-frying*

200g vermicelli
oil
2 tsp salt
*2 tsp mild curry
    powder*

1 Cook the vermicelli in boiling salted water for 5 minutes. Drain into a colander and then run it under cold water to cool it down completely. Pour a teaspoon of oil over it and mix with your hands so that all the vermicelli is coated. This is to stop it from sticking together.

2 Lay it out on a paper towel and cover it with another layer of paper towel.

3 Pour oil into the saucepan until it is about 7 cm deep. Heat the oil so that it is hot enough for a small piece of vermicelli to sizzle and float to the top if you put it in.

4 Lay out more paper towel ready next to the saucepan you are going to use to deep-fry.

5 Mix together the salt and curry powder and set aside.

6 Add a tangle of vermicelli to the oil. As soon as it hits the oil it will sizzle and spit and rise to the top. Carefully turn it over with the slotted spoon, leave for 1-2 minutes and then take out and place on the paper towel (it should not be brown, just stiff) and sprinkle with a large pinch of the salt and curry powder mix. Continue until all the vermicelli is used up.

Sherbet Slurpers

...there were Nishnobblers and Gumglotters and Blue Bubblers and
<u>Sherbet Slurpers</u> and Tongue Rakers, and as well as all this, there was
a whole lot of splendid stuff from the great Wonka factory itself.
THE GIRAFFE AND THE PELLY AND ME

You might want to put your laboratory coat on for this recipe – it's
more of a chemistry process than a cooking one! Once the mixture is
made it is scooped into straws, which are then sealed – the perfect
size to stash in a pocket for an emergency slurp...

MAKES 5

You will need:

5 plastic straws
1 lighter
1 adult
1 piece of paper
½ tsp of citric acid
  (available from
  chemists)
4 Lucozade glucose
  energy tablets,
  crushed to a fine
  powder
¼ tsp bicarbonate
  of soda
1-2 tsp of
  icing sugar

1 Ask an adult to seal the end of all the straws by
melting one end of the straw and then pressing it together
with his/her fingers. The plastic does get hot, so the
lighter should be held to it for just a couple of seconds
before the edges are pressed together.

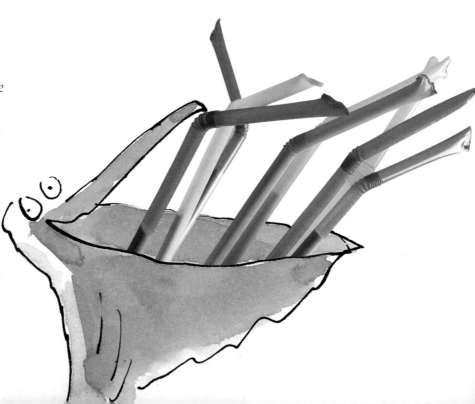

2 Mix together the first 3 ingredients and then add 1 tsp of the icing sugar. Taste it before you add more, as this may already be sweet enough for you. Don't add too much, as the fizz will disappear.

3 Fold a large piece of paper and then pour the Slurper mix into the fold. Get it into the straw by scooping the straw along through the mix and tapping the sealed end on the surface you're working on between each scoop.

4 As each one is filled, ask the adult to seal the other end in the same way as before. When you are ready to slurp your sherbet, open up one end of the straw and insert into mouth.

Bean's Cider

"You're poaching," shrieked Rat.
"Put that down at once! There'll be
none left for me!" Rat was perched
upon the highest shelf in the cellar, peering
out from behind a huge jar.
There was a small rubber tube inserted
in the neck of the jar, and Rat was
using this tube to suck out the cider.

FANTASTIC MR FOX

SERVES 1

You will need:

peeler
apple corer
food processor
fine mesh sieve
small saucepan
strong arms

4 apples – a sweet variety
1 lime, squeezed
2 tbsp light muscovado sugar
1 cinnamon stick, broken
  into 3 pieces
1 carton of apple juice

1 Peel and core the apples.

2 Place in the food processor with lime juice and purée for 4 minutes.

3 Push through a very fine sieve into a small saucepan.

4 Add the muscovado sugar and the broken cinnamon stick.

5 Heat gently while stirring.

6 Push through a sieve again – if it is too thick, add some apple juice.

7 Pour into a mug and it's ready.

Devil's Drenchers

When you have sucked a Devil's Drencher for a
minute or so, you can set your breath alight and blow
a huge column of fire twenty feet into the air.

THE GIRAFFE AND THE PELLY AND ME

The great thing about a Devil's Drencher is that it is two recipes in one. When you first make it, you eat it with a spoon and if it melts before you finish it, it magically transforms into a delicious drink which you can suck through a straw.

SERVES 1

You will need:

1 long wooden skewer
liquidiser or food processor

6 liquorice laces
9 strawberry laces
250g frozen raspberries
    (you can freeze the
    berries yourself or
    buy them frozen)
250g frozen cranberries
juice of 3 oranges
6 tbsp icing sugar

1 Tightly twist all the liquorice laces and 6 of the strawberry laces around the wooden skewer. Squish them together at the top.

2 Cut the remaining laces in half and drape over the top of the skewer. You will need to balance this in a glass while you make the quenching Drencher.

3 Place all remaining ingredients in the food processor or liquidiser and process until smooth.

4 Quickly spoon into another glass and spear in the laced skewer.

5 Eat or drink.

NB. This mixture can be sieved if you don't like the seeds.

Liquid Chocolate Mixed by Waterfall

Charlie put the mug to his lips, and as the rich warm creamy chocolate ran down his throat into his empty tummy, his whole body from head to toe began to tingle with pleasure, and a feeling of intense happiness spread over him.

CHARLIE AND THE CHOCOLATE FACTORY

SERVES 1

You will need:

rolling pin
saucepan
whisk

100g milk chocolate
100ml milk
1 Cadbury's Flake

1 While the chocolate is still in its packaging, batter it with a rolling pin.

2 Put the chocolate bits into a saucepan and add the milk. Stir over a low heat until all the chocolate is melted.

3 Whisk the mixture to make it frothy and then pour it into the biggest mug you can find.

4 Use the Flake as a stirrer.

Fizzy Lifting Drinks

"Oh, those are fabulous!" cried Mr Wonka. "They fill you with bubbles, and the bubbles are full of a special kind of gas, and this gas is so terrifically lifting that it lifts you right off the ground just like a balloon, and up you go until your head hits the ceiling – and there you stay."

"But how do you come down again?" asked little Charlie.

"You do a burp, of course," said Mr Wonka.

CHARLIE AND THE CHOCOLATE FACTORY

SERVES 1

You will need:

cream soda
vanilla ice cream

1 Close all the doors so that you don't end up on the moon.
2 Pour cream soda into a glass.
3 Top with a giant scoop of vanilla ice cream.
4 Drink.
5 Burp.

Blue Bubblers

THE GIRAFFE AND THE PELLY AND ME

So, it's the grown-ups' cocktail hour and you're not sure what to drink yourself. Here is the answer.

SERVES 1

You will need:

1 large glass
1 long wooden
  skewer

juice of 2 lemons
1 litre of sparkling
  water
caster sugar to taste
blue food colouring
6 blueberries
6 blackberries

1 Squeeze lemons, add the juice to the sparkling water and add sugar until it's sweet enough for you.

2 Add enough food colouring so that it is the perfect shade of blue (you won't need a lot).

3 Carefully thread the berries onto the skewers – alternating between the blueberries and the blackberries. The length of your skewer will depend on the height of your glass.

4 Place the skewer into the glass and let cocktail time officially begin...